DG'z Notebook
My Path to the Groove - Ideas from a Beat Collector

NOTEBOOK
5.5 x 8.5 — 120 PAGES

MADE IN U.S.A.

By David Garibaldi

Edited by Joe Bergamini

Produced by Rob Wallis

Cover + book design by Mike Hoff

Music engraving by David Garibaldi

Video and audio recording and photography by Phil Hawkins - pnotemedia.com

© 2022 Hudson Music, LLC

Video Lesson Access
Visit HudsonMusic.com/register to register and view the DG'z Notebook video lessons.

Registration Code:
DG-8H3NZ63X

See page 5 of this book for additional informtaion.

DG'z NOTEBOOK
CONTENTS

INTRODUCTION	4
DEDICATION	5
ABOUT THE MEDIA	5
DEVELOPMENT OF THE TWO SOUND LEVELS	6
DRUM KEY	6
THE JAM W/P.M.E.	7
A FUNKY GOOD SHUFFLE	11
4 FOUR	19
A SICK 6	23
SECRETS OF 6/8: FOUR GROOVES	25
THE FUNKY FOOT(S)	31
FUTURE SOUNDS UPDATE:	
PERMUTATION STUDY #13.1	37
PERMUTATION STUDY #13.2	43
2000 EE-LEVIN: ODD TIME IN 4/4	47
THE EAST BAY 13'z	55
DG'z RESOURCE LIST	65
ABOUT THE AUTHOR	68

Introduction

One of the most valuable study tools I use to develop my vocabulary is my notebook. In my practice sessions, I get all sorts of musical ideas. When I come across something that lights up my brain, I write it down, and always date the page. Sometimes I'll revisit an idea and develop it further, or leave it alone and move on.

My thinking here is if it has been such rich resource in my creative process, why not put together a book that illustrates this idea? I encourage my students to start a notebook, and that it's a path to developing a voice. One thing is for sure, if you give it a chance, it works.

My "mission" has been to make my musical journey as creative as possible. I want my music to be personal and have a signature, which is what inspires and drives me.

Part of my study is building my brain. As I've gotten older, I've come to realize the importance of mindset, and how important it is in my continued development as a player and teacher, but also as a person, father, husband, and friend. The principles of success are the same in any field of life, only the context in which they are applied is different.

All throughout our lives, we are surrounded by people who have achieved success in spite of the odds and the challenges they have faced. How do they do it? We also know people who started out with only a dream and nothing else, then achieved success—maybe you're one of them, or maybe you want to be one of them. I believe that becoming an elite performer in any area of life is attainable by nothing other than simply hard work. It starts with a thought, getting excited, and then builds from there. This thought then becomes your vision, your driving force. Take action or else nothing happens—the dream remains a dream.

As a young person, 17 years old, I had a very clear "vision" of what I wanted to become, and that is what I'm still pursuing today. One of my favorite inspirational quotes is by Mark Twain: "Don't let school get in the way of your education." Once I began creating with what I was learning, my voice began to emerge.

If you act on your dream, understanding that your will is your power, that becomes the fuel that helps to propel you down your path. I've learned that motivation is something that I do, not something that I am. If you're going to wait until you feel the urge, then the success you seek will never happen. The secret, if there is one, is to get to work—every day, work at what you want to happen; every day, turn your dream into action, and never let circumstances dictate how you think.

Another one of my favorite quotes is "Genius is persistence in disguise." Excellence is available to anyone who takes ownership of their path and gets to work. Don't allow yourself to become discouraged. I've read that everything can be figured out. If someone has done it, then it's doable. To me, this makes complete sense. What is it that you want to achieve? What's your dream?

There are many great books available today to help you build what you want, that help you to build your brain. These kinds of books are essential and should be on the shelf alongside *Stick Control* or *Master Studies*. The ones that speak to you are the ones that you keep in your library. Turn your practice room into a research library; have in it everything you need to help you focus on where you want to go. Be yourself.

Are you ready? Let's get started!

David Garibaldi
Livermore, CA
September 9, 2021

Dedication

To my teachers: Chandler Henderson, Jim Campana, Anthony Caviglia, Gene Graves, Chuck Brown, Richard Wilson, Murray Spivack and Bruce Becker... thank you for a lifetime full of learning your lessons.

About the Media

This book includes online access to video lessons, to help you practice each lesson along with DG.

Each lesson has with sheet music featuring a scrolling cursor so you can learn at your own pace. This creates an ideal practice tool to master the concepts in the book, regardless of your playing level or music-reading experience.

To access these video lessons, visit HudsonMusic.com/register and register your product using the unique access code found in the front of this book.

A free HudsonMusic.com account will be required to register and access the video lessons. If you do not already have a HudsonMusic.com account, you can create an account during registration on our website. Once inside the online book media, the lessons are titled to match the chapters in the book.

Development of the Two Sound Levels with the Hands

The hi-hat, snare drum and bass drum are the three basic drum-set components used in many modern drumming styles. Having an understanding of how these voices interact with each other is an important key in building a powerful vocabulary. This graph illustrates the dynamic distances between these three voices in a groove setting.

These levels are always controlled by the overall dynamic level of the music being played. In a normal playing situation the rimshot may or may not be forte (f). This is determined by the situation. The graph illustrates the differences in the two levels and most recordings will reflect what is seen here.

Developing this concept will improve the overall sound of your playing and should be considered a fundamental drum set technique. I explain this in detail in *Future Sounds* pages 5-7. The most important aspect of this is the texture and lightness of the ghosted notes. By definition, ghost notes are to be transparent. The snare drum ghosted notes are to be blended with the hi-hat so that the two sounds are almost indistinguishable from one another. Think of

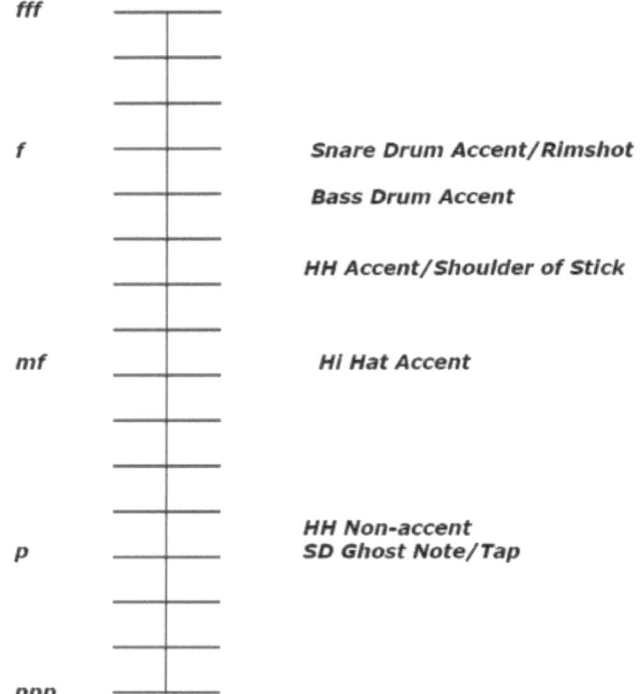

a small shaker; the ghosted snare drum notes and hi-hat replicate this sound, and if done correctly, will have a shaker-like quality that weaves itself in and throughout your grooves. Over time, this sound will permeate your playing.

DG'z Ultimate Drum Key

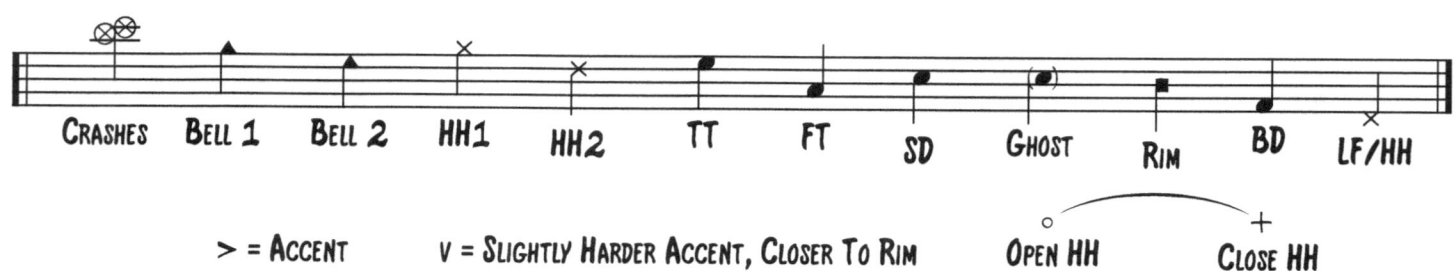

THE JAM w/ P.M.E.

The Jam w/P.M.E.

This collection of beats comes from my practice sessions playing along with Peter Michael Escovedo's "Ghetto Mambo." I'm always on the lookout for music to play along with, and I find that practicing this way is the perfect musical metronome. Having inspiring music as a backdrop for my ideas shapes them in unexpected ways, much like when I'm in a live setting. I highly recommend building a practice library of music you like—no rules, it can be anything that sparks your creativity.

These beats also fit into a similar category of ideas I played on a TOP song called "Eastside"—all interchangeable. Those grooves and the "Eastside" play-along can be found in my book *The Code of Funk*. This track is also perfect to use for this study.

Try This:

Begin with Exercise 1, or any other you might want to try. Look at how the coordination works and then piece the exercise together, beat by beat, gradually connecting all the notes until you can play the entire measure. Important: Go slowly, building comfort and control. This process will show you how the parts fit together and allows for the isolation of all the coordination "problems," which will be different for everyone.

Once there's a basic understanding of what is involved, then start using a metronome.

Refer to the lesson in *Future Sounds* pages 19-20 called "Practicing an Exercise" for a system on progressively building each groove until they can be performed smoothly.

Remember to *always* have the sound levels dialed in: All the ghosted notes should have the sound and texture of a small shaker. This shaker-like sound weaves itself through each groove in between all the accented notes. Refer to the sound level graph on page 6 to understand the volume and textural differences between the hi-hat, snare drum and bass drum.

One great and very simple way to develop this perception is to get a small shaker and play a 16th-note groove. Listen to how the shaker sounds and visualize replicating this sound with hi-hat and snare drum ghost notes. It is surprisingly effective ear training.

The next step is to play with any music track of your choice. This puts each idea into a musical context, which shapes the ideas even further. The goal is to get into a flow. Always look for music to play along with, and build a list of favorites. A metronome is a very valuable practice tool, but then using a music track shapes your ideas in ways that a metronome can't. Eventually, when you're playing with other musicians, your ideas will evolve into practical skills.

Repetition is very important and will help to cement the coordination ideas into your memory.

We're building vocabulary. I want to be conversational, just like with a spoken language. Having a developed vocabulary allows me to express my ideas in many ways when presented with a context.

A final thought on repetition—this is a critical step. When I'm really working to understand something, I do it over and over again for a period of weeks or even months, sometimes years. I continually revisit the idea. Continually means over and over and over and over. Eventually, the new concept becomes part of my working knowledge.

This study is in two parts; each exercise in both parts permutates by quarter notes. Column 1 shows the exercises, while column 2 is the turnaround measure that connects to the next permutation.

The mechanism used in Part 1 is an additional

open hi-hat. Play the exercise three times, then the turnaround or transition measure once. The turnaround measure adds an open hi-hat, then subtracts it when going to the next permutation.

The mechanism in Part 2 is a two-beat turnaround. As in Part 1, play each exercise three times, then the transitional measure once.

The quarter-note permutation sequence is:

1 2 3 4
4 1 2 3
3 4 1 2
2 3 4 1

Developing vocabulary and coordination is a slow and detailed process. I'm always striving to be patient, persistent and consistent, reminding myself of these things often as I recommit each day.

Enjoy!

THE JAM w/ P.M.E.

David Garibaldi

♩ = 100

Part 1

Play groove 3x or more, then transition measure...

A Funky Good Shuffle

A Funky Good Shuffle

I love the music of James Brown. It taught me about groove and is what inspired me to start creating my musical path forward.

This beat collection is inspired by one of my fave James Brown songs, "Doing It To Death," aka "Gonna Have a Funky Good Time." The groove for the song is a shuffle. The shuffle is a huge part of the pulse of American music. Rhythmically, the basic subdivision that makes the music "shuffle" is the triplet. The great James Gadson says that a shuffle is based on 12/8—there is the definition.

When I was growing up, music was taught in school and learning was very traditional. My introduction to music was orchestra and marching band, then came jazz. Triplets are a big part of orchestral and marching band literature, so when moving into basic jazz concepts, I learned about the triplet connection to drum set. My very first paid gig was with a big band, then came rock 'n' roll.

In my experience, the triplet has proven to be a gateway to a stronger groove. Understanding and being able to smoothly play triplet ideas has made all of my 16th note playing much stronger, in that I can micro-relax the 16th-note grid and lean closer to triplets. This makes the groove swing in a way it could not if my reference for 16th-note playing was strictly "straight up and down."

I learned a lot about this particular rhythmic relationship as a member of Talking Drums. My bandmates Michael Spiro and Jesús Diaz also became my teachers. It was kind of unique situation; I was learning as I was performing. We somehow fit together perfectly, bending and blending our individual skills to fit together into a musical concept.

At first, all I could do was play my funk beats; I knew nothing about clave or how to relax my time to fit with what they were doing. Michael is American and grew up in the American musical tradition, but then fell in love with Cuban music; he can easily navigate both worlds. Jesús is Cuban and plays with a "slippery" time feel: it's very loose, but also very accurate. He and Michael play off of each other perfectly. I came from this R'n'B kind of place: having influences, but more "vertical" stylistically.

Incidentally, I initially met Michael as a student: I wanted lessons on "Latin" music, and he was the one most highly recommended by all the Bay Area musicians. Our lessons almost immediately turned into a collaboration and through him, I met Jesús. Soon after that, we all began working together.

At first, I had a very difficult time locking up with Jesús groove, because I didn't yet understand the concept of "fix." Michael, who invented the term, calls this in-between place "fix," which is the perfect description of this concept.

Fix is the ability to play in a spot that is between four (4/4) and six (6/8). This interpretation comes from Africa. In the musics of the Caribbean, Brazil, and New Orleans, the rhythms are played in this relaxed way, sometimes neither 4 or 6, but this in-between place that has a unique swing: moving somewhere between 16th notes and triplets, with a very strong quarter-note pulse.

During one of our recording sessions, I asked Jesús if he could straighten out his groove a little bit so I could lock with his parts. He replied, "You mean you don't want it to swing?" End of argument! At that moment I realized that the "problem" was me: I hadn't yet developed the perception of the rhythmic power of fix. Fix allowed me to finally lock in with him. Finally understanding this relationship has dramatically changed my ability to create in new and deeper ways.

All that being said, shuffles are in a way, a lost art.

When I was coming up, being able to play a shuffle that swung was part of a drummer's required skill set when doing gigs. This isn't as true today, unless you play in blues bands or come from parts of the country where a shuffle is part of the musical tradition. I think of Texas, Chicago or Kansas City, each place interpreting this groove in their own unique way. No matter where you come from, though, the basis of it is triplets.

In this study, the grooves are all triplet based, and the emphasis is on achieving a solid quarter-note pulse with the triplets flowing in between. Listening to the track, the guitar parts supply all the triplets, with the drums playing a version of a shuffle.

4/4 = 12/8 (2 bars of 6/8) = ♩. = Triplets = Count:

<u>1</u> & a <u>2</u> & a <u>3</u> & a <u>4</u> & a

Understanding this relationship will take you from jazz to rock and all points in between.

Photo by Martin Kleinbreuer (Yamaha Drums Europe A&R Manager)

A Funky Good Shuffle

David Garibaldi

SURPRISE...!!! OPEN-HANDED

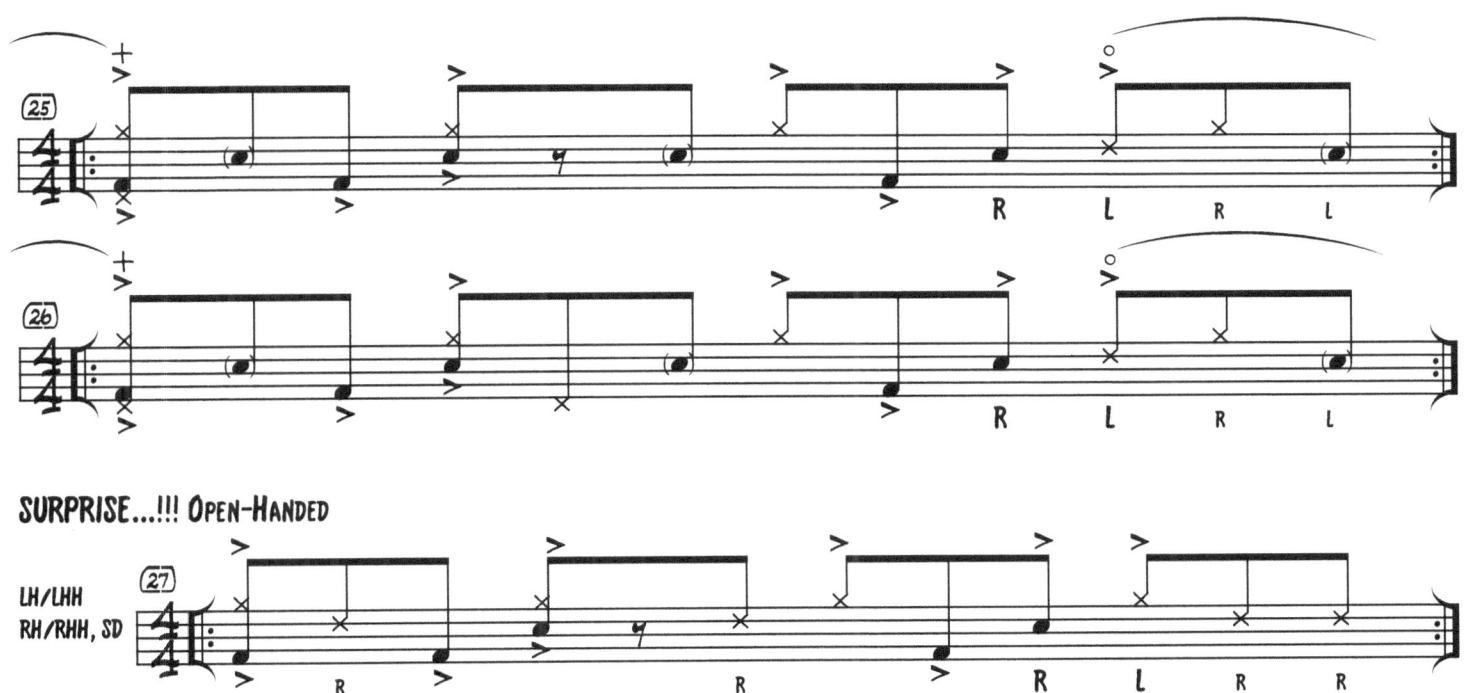

4 Four

4 Four

Beats without 2 & 4 always light up my brain. The challenge is to make a rhythm groove equally as hard as I would banging out 2 & 4. Don't get me wrong here, 2 & 4 is a very important basic part of a drummer's vocabulary—a necessary skill. But being able to expand and manipulate rhythm takes groove playing to stratospheric levels. It also becomes part of a drummer's signature. Each of us is unique and has a perspective that is ours alone. It's like handwriting: unique to the individual.

The spoken word is how we communicate our thoughts. The more expansive our vocabulary is, the more detail we can provide when we want to express ourselves. We're only limited by the size of our vocabulary. The exact same thing is true of our musical vocabulary, which has rhythmic and melodic components. We combine those when we play music. A musical context determines what we play, just like a spoken context determines what we say.

As a drummer, the more rhythm I understand, the deeper I can go when creating grooves. This isn't always complex and crazy; context determines all of it. I can go deep in subtle ways: adding or subtracting notes, voice substitutions, dynamic shading, stylistic combinations, levels of permutation, or I can go to other planets! I create *how* I want to present myself.

My first two years with Tower of Power were intense. In this period, I began developing the idea of specific beats for songs and then specific beats for sections of songs. My vocabulary began to grow in ways I didn't expect. During this time, I began to listen to Latin music, especially the music of the great Ray Barretto. I loved the sound and the flow of how everything was so rhythmically integrated and precise. The most apparent thing to my ears was that there was no drum set player, there was no 2 & 4, but the GROOVE was badass.

I had the thought that I could do this too, but with the funky beat. I knew nothing about Latin music, nothing about clave and its presence in the beats I was playing. I created something that was inspired by what I was hearing. This is how the rhythm concept for the TOP song "Soul Vaccination" was born. I was always experimenting with different ways to use all I was learning, and I have vivid memories of the rehearsals when we put that song together. We knew that we had entered a new phase in our musical journey—and this freedom became a huge part of the way we create our music, as well as what I was to do personally.

DG Rudimentz

Throughout my drum life, as I continue to build and strengthen my vocabulary, I've noticed that there are certain patterns or stickings that have become fundamental elements of how I put things together: sequences of rights and lefts that are small modules or connecting phrases—personalized rudiments. Everyone does this; it's like your way of speaking. Same thing here. We'll explore this further in other lessons.

For example, looking at Ex. 1:

Phrase #1 - Part of my vocabulary since the early '70s, and one of the first ideas that came from using permutation when I was learning the King Kong beat. Over time, this sequence has become one of my key building blocks when creating and appears in many different ways.

Phrase #2 - A slight variation of the King Kong.

Phrase #3 - My version of the King Kong beat, which was invented by drummer Pete DePoe of the band Redbone. Learning this changed my playing in a dramatic way.

Performance Notes

This study permutates by quarter notes and uses a turnaround "device" that, when added and then subtracted, resolves to the next permutation.

Play each exercise 4 times. Play the first ending 3 times, then take the second ending. The ending contains the turnaround, which is an additional open hi-hat and a slight accent change to accommodate that. Subtract the turnaround and resolve to the next permutation sequence.

The permutation sequence is as follows:

1 2 3 4
4 3 2 1
3 4 1 2
4 1 2 3

COMFORT + FLOW = GROOVE

As ALWAYS, discipline yourself to count. Once this becomes a habit, it will pay HUGE dividends.

Enjoy!

David Garibaldi

4 FOUR

♩ = 94 - 100

PERMUTATE BY 1/4 NOTES...

A Sick 6

This idea comes from a Tower of Power recording session. Our most recent releases, *The Soul Side of Town* and *Step Up*, involved recording 28 new compositions, with one week of that devoted to rhythm section jams that were to be collaboratively developed into songs.

"East Bay All Day," "You Wanna be a Winner" and "After Hours" were written from some of those jams.

A Sick 6 is a bar of 6/4 that is played over 4/4. In 4/4, this takes three measures to resolve (12 beats). Think James Brown, but slightly sideways!

Play as written or as three separate measures.

A SICK 6

DAVID GARIBALDI

♩ = 100 - 106

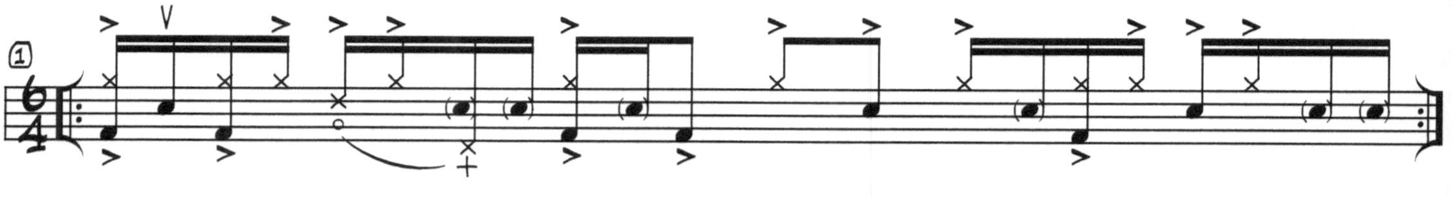

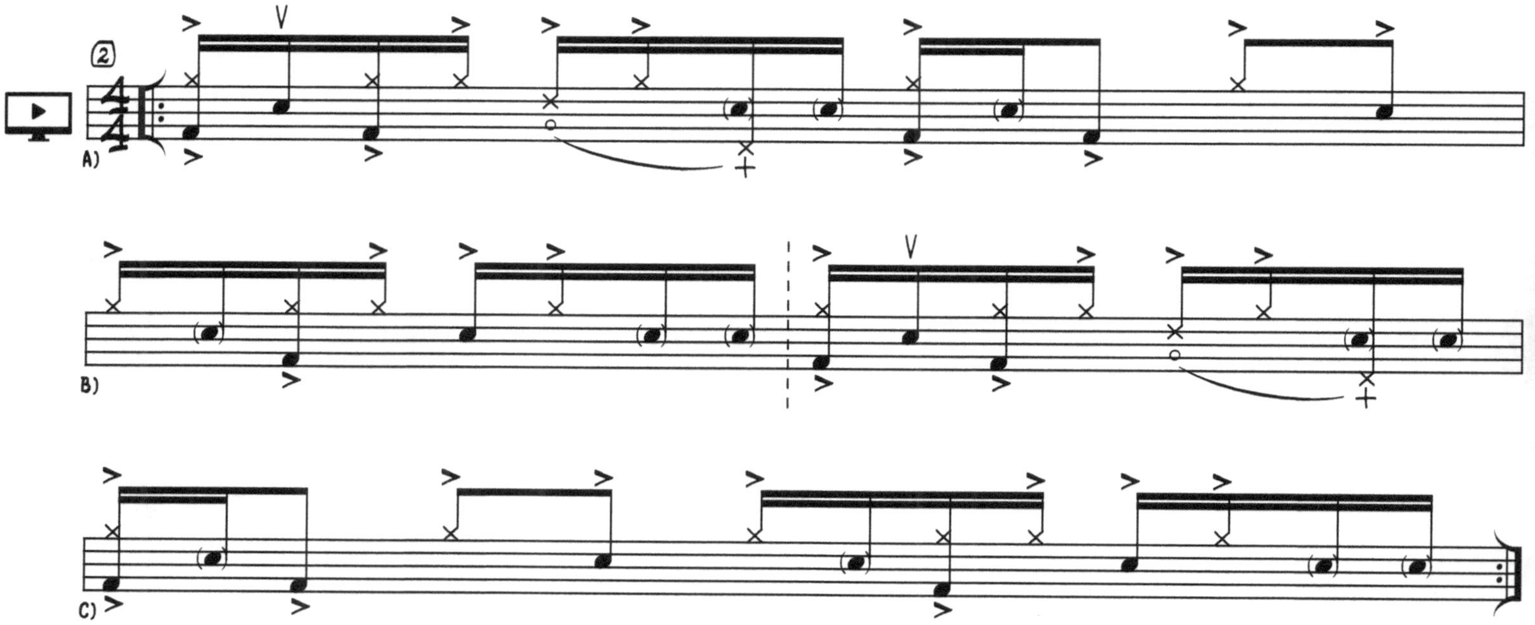

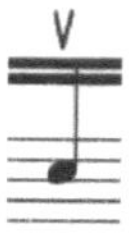

= A SLIGHTLY HARDER ACCENT, STRIKING THE SD 1/2 WAY BETWEEN THE CENTER AND RIM.

Secrets of 6/8

Secrets of 6/8: Four Grooves

In the period of time from approximately 1992-2002, I was part of the percussion trio Talking Drums. We were a co-led collective, and surprisingly never had a conflict with the arrangement. My trio mates were Michael Spiro and Jesús Diaz, two of the most creative and "gifted" musicians I've ever known. It was a special time for us—and for that reason, we've never officially broken up! The door is still open, should we decide to add another chapter to one of the most creative periods in our musical lives.

During our time together, we spent many hours rehearsing, gigging and writing. For me in particular, it was like school every day. I had never before been in a situation like that, where I could go home after every session and say that I learned something. These are my brothers, but also my teachers.

It was a ten-year period that was creative *and* prolific. We released a video and two books, which were intended to be a trilogy. Each component stands alone, but together form a solid presentation of how to apply folkloric music and traditions in a uniquely personal way—how to make something your own, while being respectful to its history.

One rhythmic area that we explored in our music was 6/8. In the Afro-Cuban tradition, 6/8 is powerful. Many of the songs in the Santeria and Abacuá literature are in 6/8. There are other forms as well, all with their own specific songs, instruments and traditions.

I was a 100% rookie when we started and for me, this was a very steep learning curve. The one thing in my favor was that creating is probably my greatest strength. So I learned as I went along, and built a path forward for myself to navigate my way through this new challenge.

We were two hand drummers and a drum set player, so my role and task was to add the missing hand drum part, but also to integrate it into my drum set parts. I created parts that melded all that together. This study comes from what I learned in that situation.

Guiro, Bembé, Rumba Columbia, Abacuá, Arará, Palo, as well as many Bátá rhythms are amongst the many African-based folkloric styles that feature 6/8. These rhythms, which are very melodic, can be simple or complex, and are performed on a variety of percussion instruments. Traditionally, the drum set isn't included, so any drum set applications must be invented. My concept of this is to take some of the traditional percussion parts or concepts and combine them with hi-hat, snare drum, and bass drum to create funk beats. In the 6/8 context, I create grooves with triplets instead of 16th notes.

The following study is based on one idea, and then expanded rhythmically and melodically by using the permutation concept. Each example includes the 6/8 clave rhythm to illustrate how each groove fits with clave, and is intended to be used for reference.

Ex. 1: This is the basic idea. This example shows the counting system, the triplet, clave, and the drum set groove. The right hand is playing the **first** note of the triplet on the hi-hat or rim of the snare drum.

- RH/HH or rim of the snare drum (the rim replicates the sound of a stick on the side of a conga drum).
- LH/bell, hi-hat, snare drum
- RF/bass drum
- LF/hi-hat

Ex. 2: This example shows the counting system, the triplet, clave, and the drum set groove. Everything permutates to the right by one eighth note. All the voices move; the right hand is playing the **second**

note of the triplet on the hi-hat or rim of the snare drum.

Ex. 3: This example shows the counting system, the triplet, clave, and the drum set groove. Everything permutates to the right by one eighth note. All the voices move; the right hand is playing the **third** note of the triplet on the hi-hat or rim of the snare drum.

Ex. 4: This is an adaptation of something I played on the Tower of Power song "Pocketful of Soul." It's the same groove, counted in the same way, but permutated from the original and repurposed for this collection of ideas.

A word about the counting system: This study is written in 6/8; clave is two bars, equaling 12/8 or 4/4. Our contemporary music system is basically 4/4, so counting this in 4/4 as triplets can be easier based on what we're used to. All of this is hybrid anyway, so use whatever works!

Performance Notes

- Counting aloud is essential in building the ability to hear the permutations in relation to where beat one is, as well as clave.

- The basic pulse is the same as a blues shuffle, except that you are using all of the triplets to build the grooves.

- Repetition (very important key!): Repeat Ex. 1 until you can count comfortably while playing it. Then move to Ex. 2., etc. In the accompanying video, when playing the form on pages 2 & 3, I don't repeat grooves 1-3. In your practice, observe the written repeats and play as many times as you like.

- Sing clave while you play the exercises.

- Try the following with the right hand:

    1. Instead of playing the hi-hat with right hand, substitute a bell.

    2. Alternate the right hand part between hi-hat and rim of the snare drum, or hi-hat and bell.

        - Bell on beat 1, hi-hat or rim on beat 2.

        - Hi-hat or rim on beat 1, bell on beat 2.

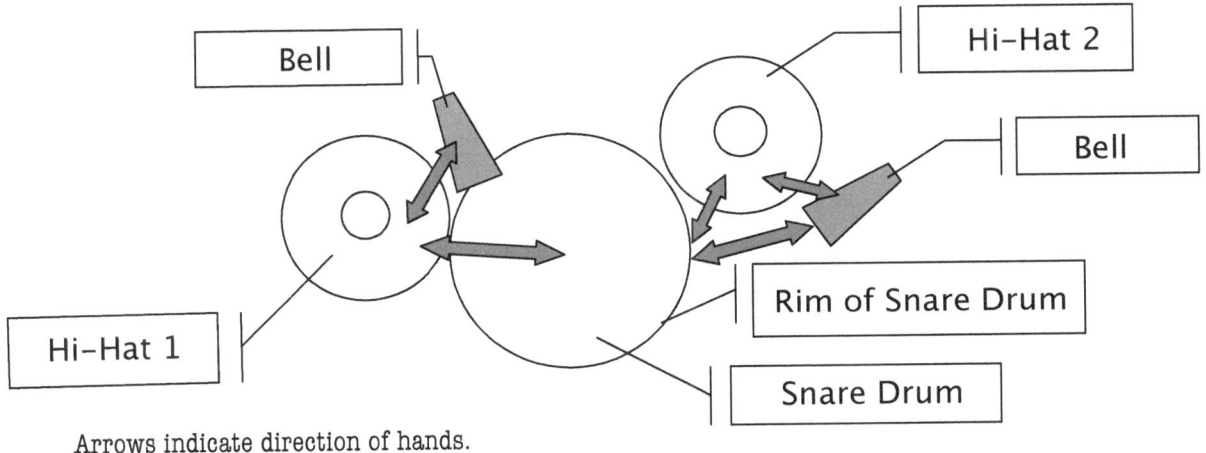

Arrows indicate direction of hands.

Secrets of 6/8
Four Grooves

David Garibaldi

♩. = 110

Groove 1

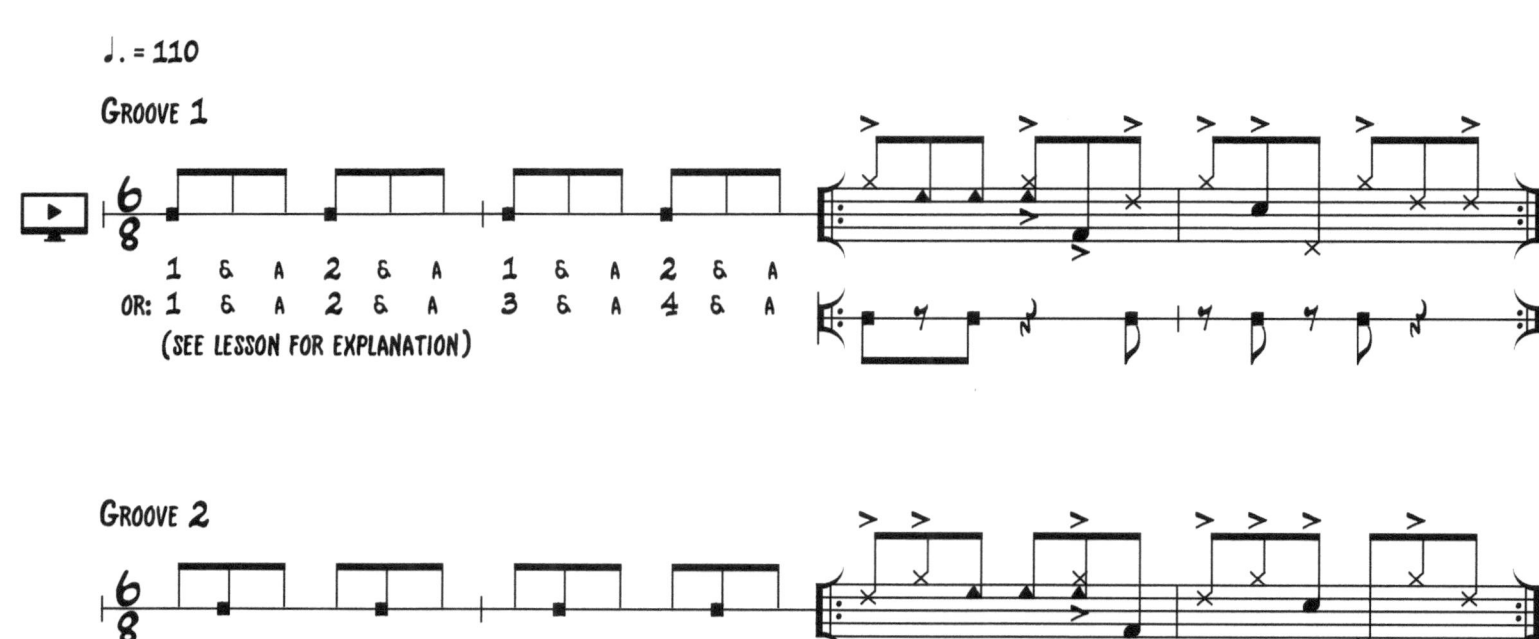

1 & a 2 & a   1 & a 2 & a
or: 1 & a 2 & a   3 & a 4 & a
(see lesson for explanation)

Groove 2

1 & a 2 & a   1 & a 2 & a
1 & a 2 & a   3 & a 4 & a

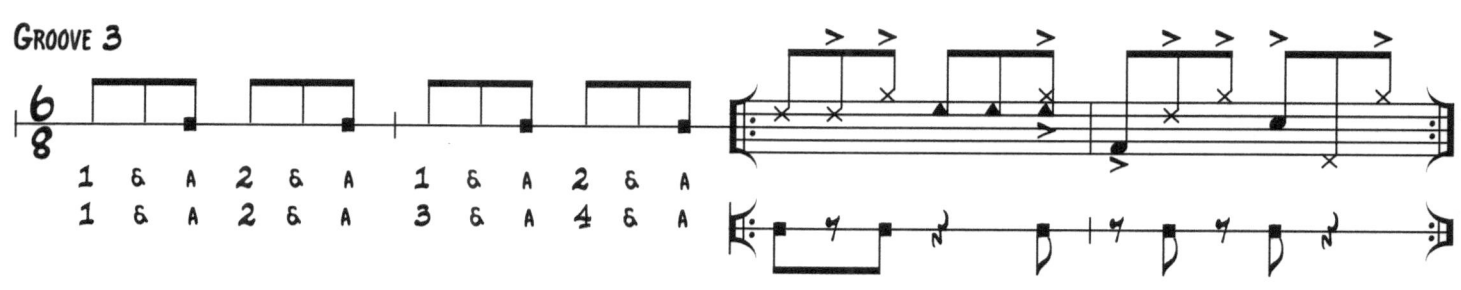

Groove 3

1 & a 2 & a   1 & a 2 & a
1 & a 2 & a   3 & a 4 & a

Groove 4

Secrets of 6/8 - Four Grooves (cont.)

Secrets of 6/8 - Four Grooves (cont.)

The Funky Foot(s)

The Funky Foot(s)

This study is built around four phrases that permutate. I put this together as a simple way to build foot strength and to clean up my double strokes. The exercises are very common, but also very effective in building precision and accuracy.

Here's the original handwritten idea from my practice notebook:

As I looked through my past note-keeping, I found that this first appeared in 2012, then showed up a couple of more times like this. It was as if it was asking to be developed into something more!

This is with stickings added to the permutations:

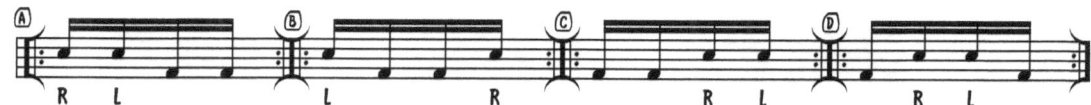

Eventually, after many visits to these combinations, I looked at the four permutations and thought they'd be a cool sounding linear groove—right hand hi-hat, left hand snare drum—a little tweak here and there, and a great sounding beat appeared!

I then began playing this instead of just the original SD/BD combinations and discovered that it was very effective in developing foot accuracy and precision in a very musical way.

Practice Suggestions

This study is in three parts: Part 1 is the initial idea, Part 2 incorporates the left-foot hi-hat, and Part 3 uses a "mechanism" to go through the permutations without using an eighth-note groove in between each one.

Try playing Ex. A-D individually, five minutes or so each, moving to the next without stopping. Experiment with various tempos—whatever challenges you. I started at 80 BPM. The idea is comfort and control.

Next, combine Ex. A-D to create a 4/4 measure with hands on snare drum and/or tom-tom. Again, do many repetitions!

A-D = 1 quarter note each; permutate by quarter notes. Counting is an important step now and will act as a compass, as well as train your ears to hear these rhythmic shifts.

1. A B C D
2. D A B C
3. C D A B
4. B C D A

Move to Exercise 1, which applies voice substitutions with the hands (RH/HH, LH/SD). Pay attention to the ghosted note and adhere to the sound level concepts. This will be a challenge as you begin moving through the permutations.

Part 1 - Ex. 2-5: The form here is similar to what is in *Future Sounds*. Six measures: Two measures of eighth-note time, then each permutation for four bars. Of course, you can play any number of measures you like. The idea is to go back and forth from eighth-note time to 16th-note time, advancing through each permutation comfortably.

||:   Time   :||:   Ex. 2 - 5   :||

BONUS 1! Omit the eighth-note timekeeping measure and play each permutation for four measures, moving to the next without stopping.

BONUS 2! Play each permutation as one measure, connecting them to create a four-measure phrase.

Part 2 - Ex. 6: Substitute left-foot hi-hat for bass drum in permutation D, as written in the exercise. Use the same form as in Part 1.

Part 3 - Ex. 7-10: Permutation A, which is bracketed in the exercise, is used as a turnaround by adding it and then subtracting it. This automatically resolves to the next quarter-note permutation in the sequence and keeps the 16th-note flow going throughout. The form here is four measures: Three measures of the exercise, then the one-measure turnaround.

||:   Exercise 3 measures   :|| Turnaround measure ||

Counting is VERY IMPORTANT! This is your compass when using permutation. As you move away from where you start, your ears can get tricked very easily. Counting helps us to keep our eyes and ears on the quarter note and especially beat one. The goal is to own the time and counting helps us to do this. Bands that play well together *own* their groove. ***Count!***

The Funky Foot(s)

♩ = 90 - 126

David Garibaldi

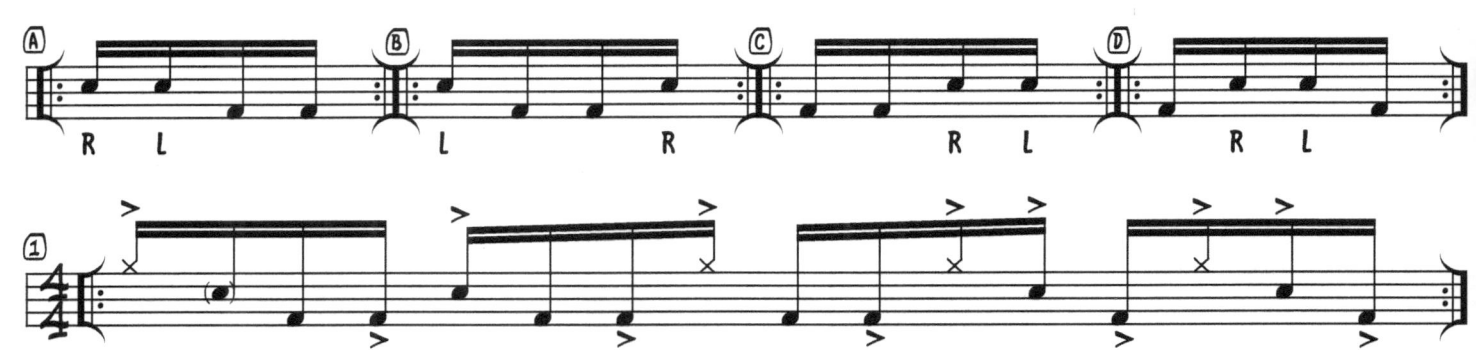

Time: 2x - Exercise: 4x

Part 1
Permutate by 1/4 notes

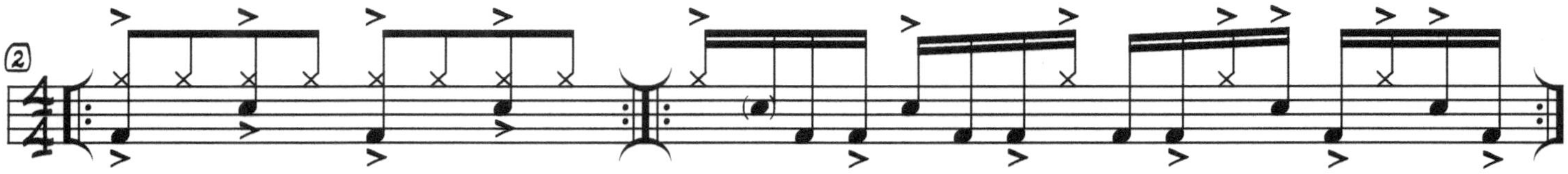

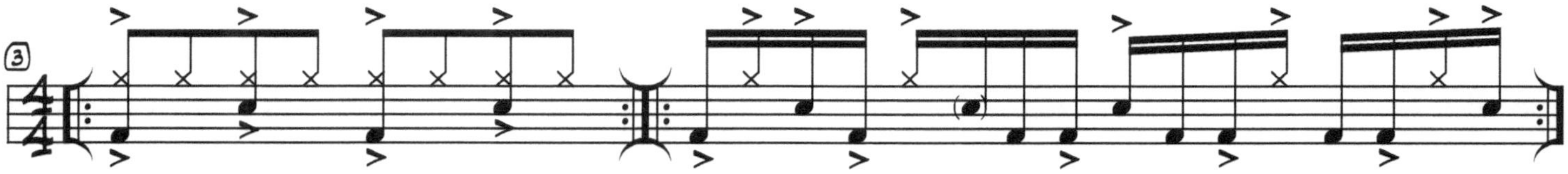

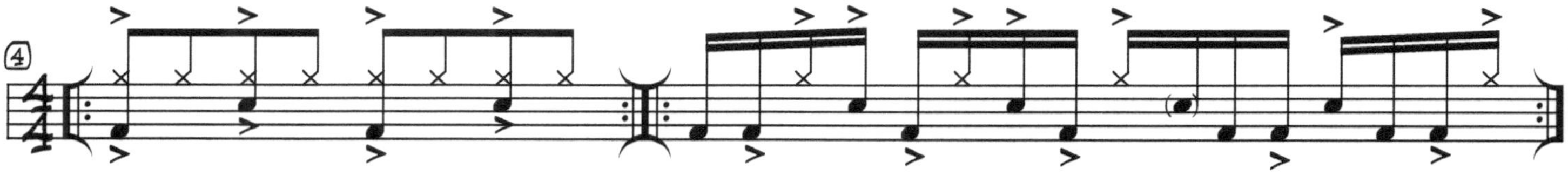

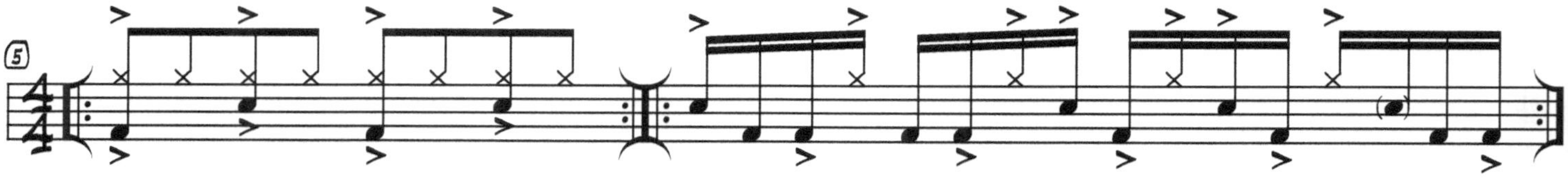

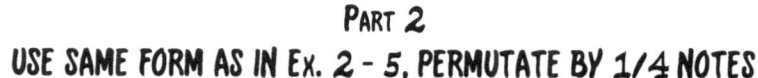

Part 2
Use same form as in Ex. 2 - 5, permutate by 1/4 notes

(Substitute LF/HH for RF/BD)

The Funky Foot(s) (cont.)

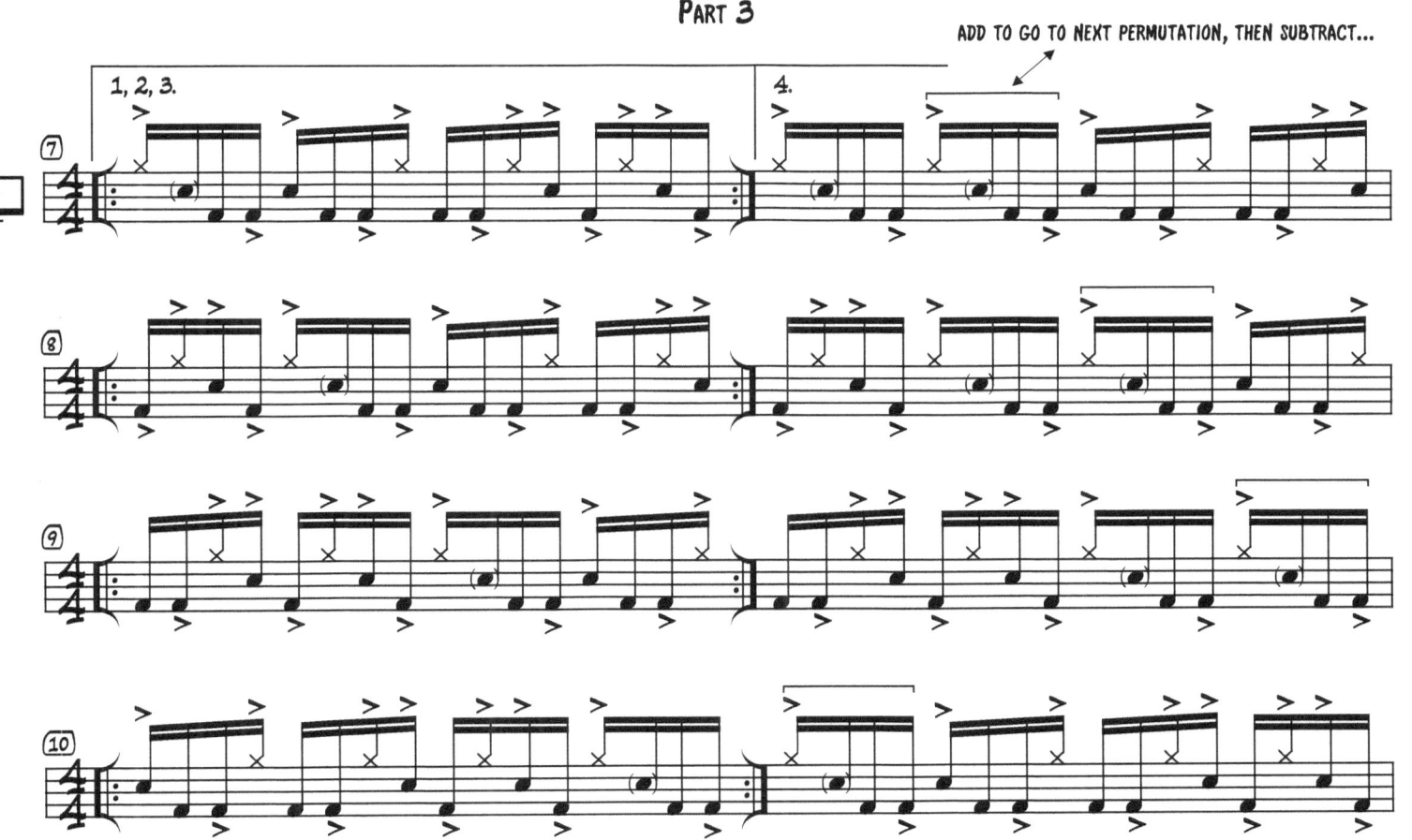

Future Sounds Update: Permutation Study #13.1

Future Sounds page 35 is my favorite in the book, and it's time for an update. I use *Future Sounds* when teaching and there's always a new twist or turn that makes the exercises a bit different and challenging in unusual directions. A note changed here and there gives new life to the material. I've never really documented all the different ways it has expanded, but knew I would at some point. We can call this *Future Sounds 2.0*.

The great thing about all of this is that the book keeps growing and changing to go along with my growth and deeper rhythmic understanding. It's all a work in progress.

This study is based on triplets and is one that I've learned a lot from. It's a beat that has given me an understanding of how much variety and unexplored territory there is with triplet groove playing. A huge moment of clarity came when I used this groove in the Talking Drums composition "Ochosi." It fit perfectly, and also fit with all kinds of other different 6/8 rhythms. Using the permutations took things into a deep place when combined with the concept of clave.

Further explanation is available in the Talking Drums trilogy: *TimbaFunk*, *Tiempo*, and the accompanying DVD, *Talking Drums*.

Here's how this update works:

In *Future Sounds*, there are 12 permutations, bridged by a triplet-based groove. The form for the study is four or eight bars of any exercise, followed by four or eight bars of a 2 & 4 triplet groove—basically continuous playing, but with alternating time feels.

For this version of the study, there are the same 12 permutations, but instead of an alternating time feel as in *Future Sounds*, there's what I call a turnaround measure that resolves to the next permutation. In this instance, it's the addition of one bass drum note in the exercise that is played one time, then subtracted; the result is the next measure in the permutation sequence.

The form can be any length. For example, play in eight-bar sections: Exercise 1 for seven measures, then the turnaround measure once. Use this form for the entire study. The length can be any number, and when you want to get to the next permutation, use the turnaround. Everything is the same as originally in *Future Sounds*, but now with the addition of one note.

The turnaround measure creates a new challenge: You're now playing a continuous linear triplet flow, with no change in the time feel.

$4/4 = 12/8$ or $\quarternote = \dottedquarternote$ = Count triplets:

1 & a **2** & a **3** & a **4** & a

Counting is very important; it puts all the notes in the right place and synchronizes mind and body. Don't underestimate its power! Once you understand its value in the learning process, you'll never look back.

Sound Levels/Ghost Notes

This is critical: the ghosted notes between the hi-hat and snare drum should have a shaker-like quality. This shaker sound weaves itself in and around all the accented notes. The challenge here is to play these notes as lightly as possible, replicating this shaker sound. I have a small shaker in my studio that I sometimes will play and as I'm doing this, I'm listening and memorizing the sound. I do this periodically because the more clearly I understand this sound, the better I can reproduce this texture in my grooves.

Here's an exercise for developing a smooth and

accurate perception of triplets, using accents and ghosted notes. It's very simple, just two sound levels. The ghosted notes *must* be played very softly (pianissimo).

Triplet Flow

This is an adaptation of an exercise I learned from the great Murray Spivack that features Moeller up and down strokes. The simplicity here is very effective in teaching this concept and is very helpful when applying it to hi-hat and snare drum.

There's much more to come. Enjoy!

PERMUTATION STUDY #13.1

David Garibaldi

Future Sounds Update, p.35

♩ = ♩. = 90-100

* ADD A NOTE (GOES TO THE NEXT PERMUTATION)

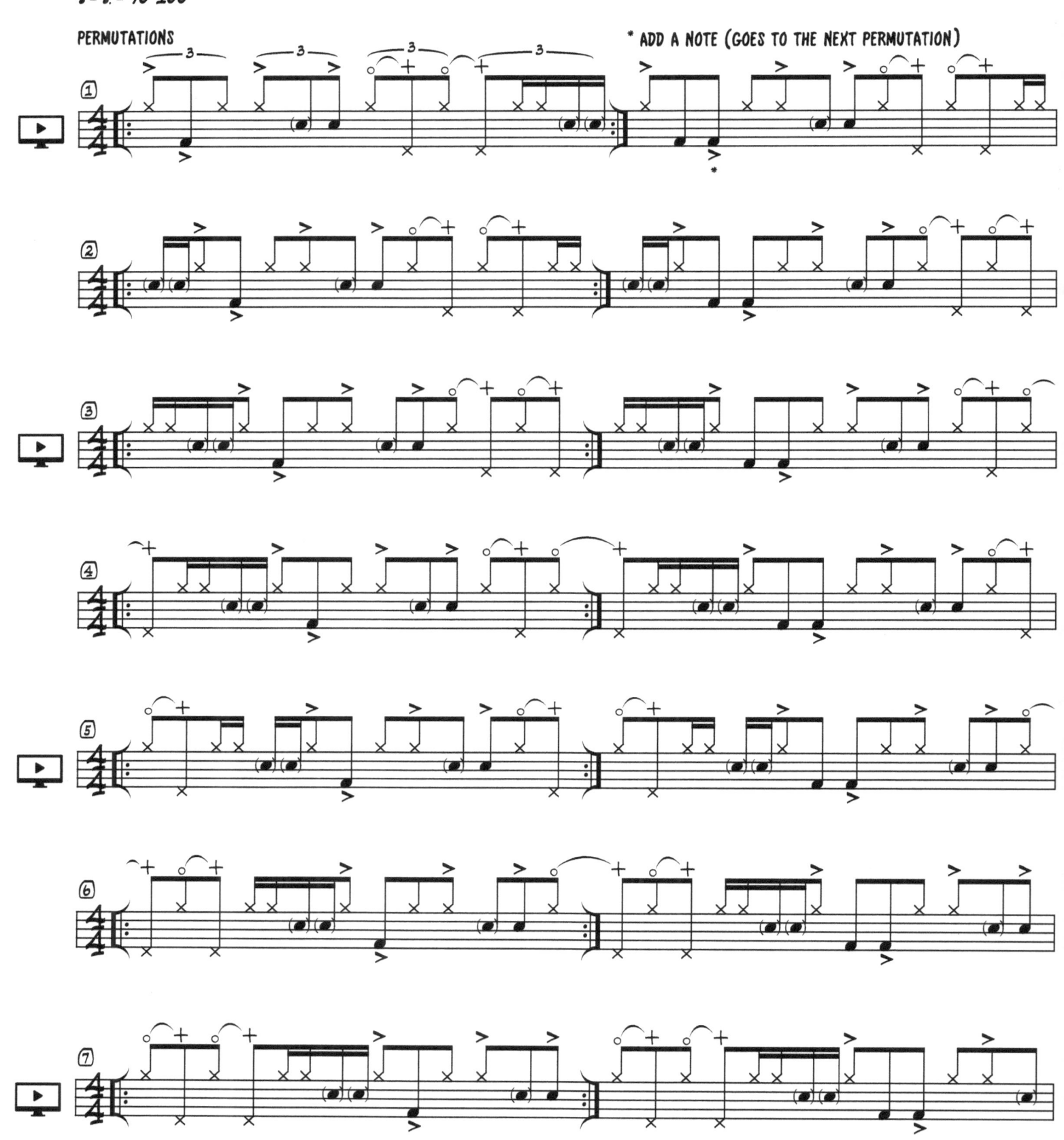

Permutation Study #13.1 (cont.)

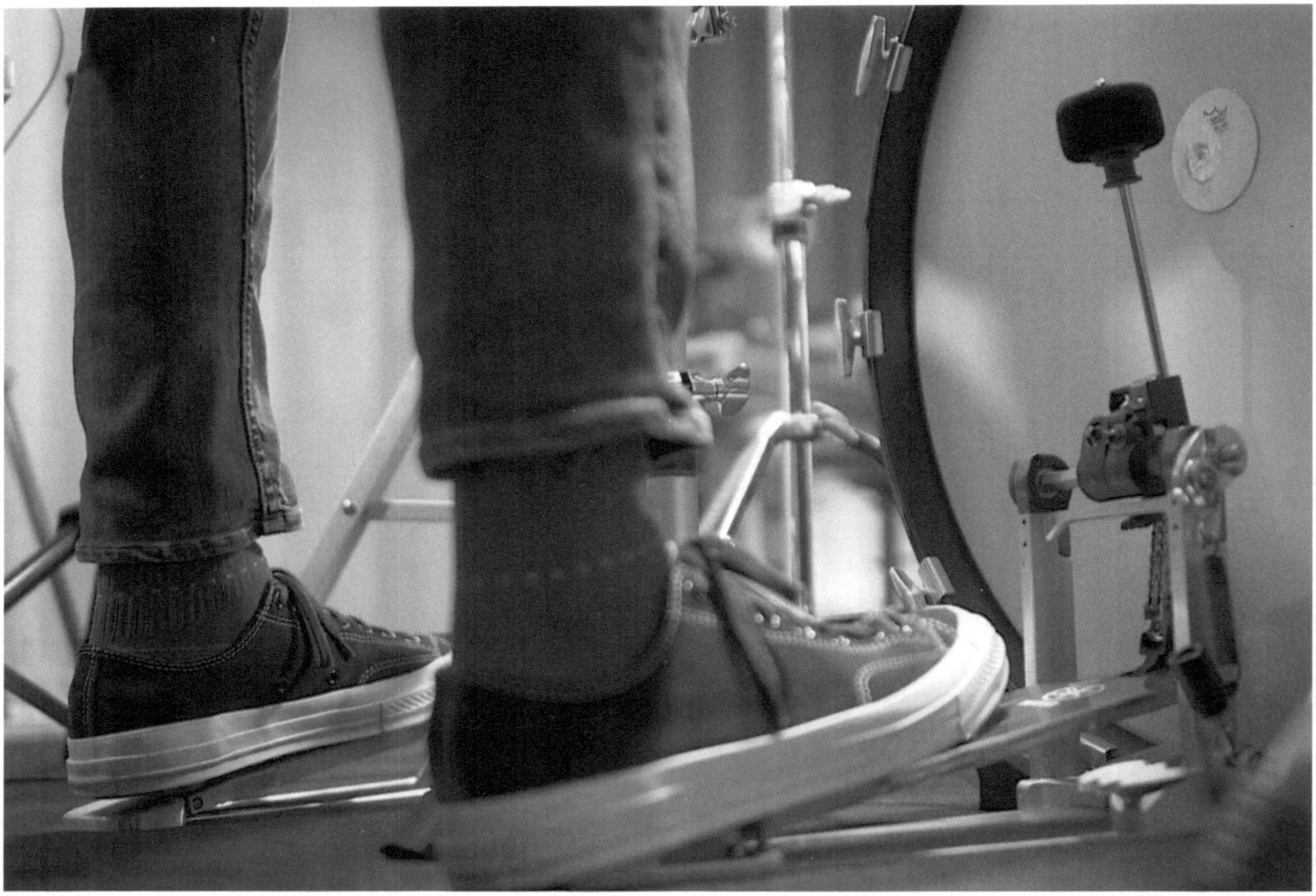

SABIAN

YAMAHA
HANDCRAFTED DRUM
CUSTOM MODEL
MADE IN JAPAN

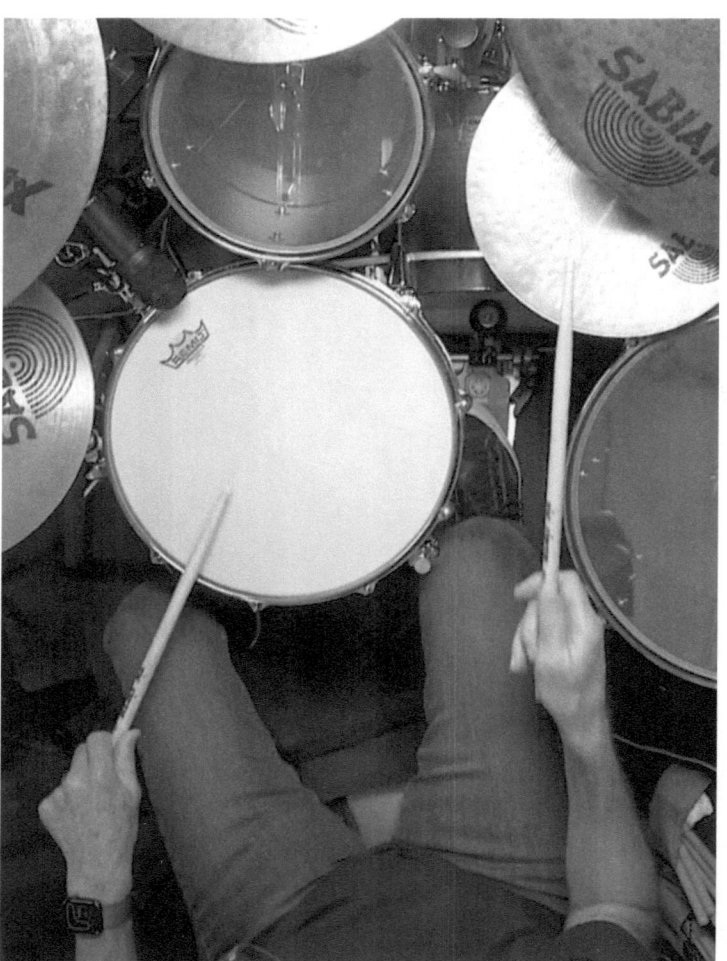

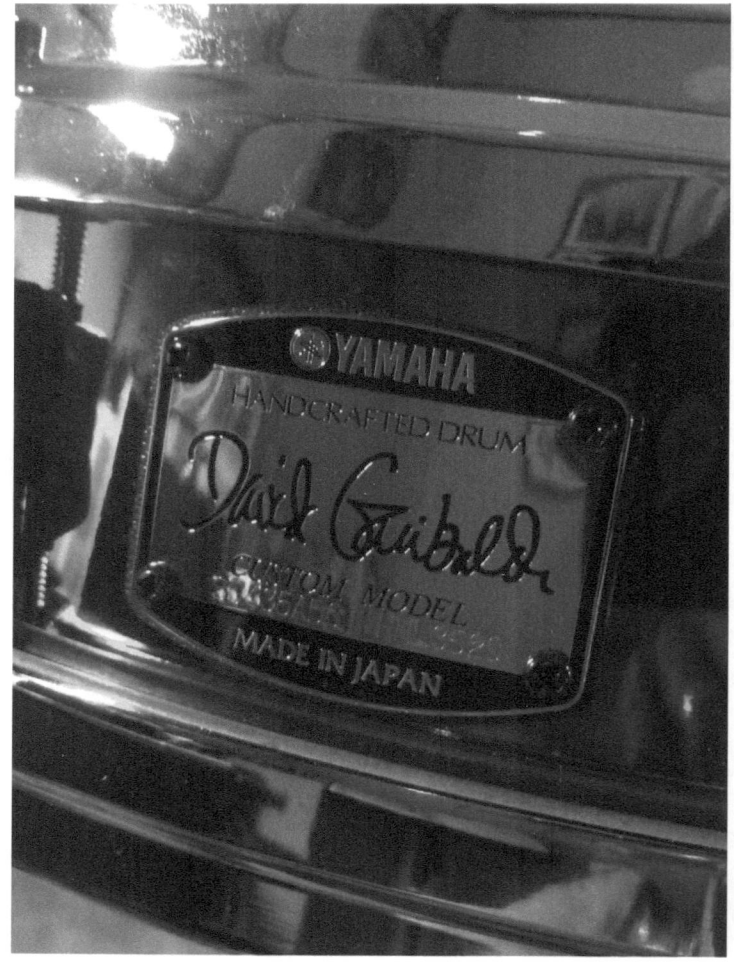

Future Sounds Update
— Permutation Study #13.2 —

Future Sounds Update: Permutation Study #13.2

Let's take a look at the "turnaround" idea from Permutation Study #13.1. By adding one note to exercise 1, which is twelve notes, this 12/8 measure now becomes a 13-note phrase: 13/8. (Played as written, it's a measure of 13/8.)

I was never that interested in playing odd times, because in most of the situations I was in, the music was in common time (4/4) and that's where I was focused. But when I realized that I could play odd times within 4/4, and saw what the potential for groove-making was, I immediately started to experiment. This concept and permutation have become key ingredients in building my vocabulary.

I apply these both in a 16th-note or triplet context. Learning how to do this has taken quite a bit of time, but has been absolutely worth the effort. The result is that I no longer look at bar lines as restrictive; I know they're there, but can now play longer phrases of unusual lengths that cross these "barriers" in some very crazy ways. I now have a growing and expanding perception of how to use this idea with a bigger picture of the possibilities that exist within 4/4.

Performance Notes

- Measure A is the 13-note phrase (13/8).

- Measures 1-13 are the 13-note phrase within 4/4 or 12/8. The dashed line delineates the beginning of each 13/8 sequence. The 13/8 note phrase within 12/8 takes 13 measures to resolve back to beat one.

- 4/4 (♩) = 12/8 (♩.): Three eighth notes per dotted quarter note.

- A dotted quarter note is the basic pulse.

- Count triplets: __1__ & a __2__ & a __3__ & a __4__ & a

- Play each measure separately and then begin connecting each measure in the sequence.

PERMUTATION STUDY #13.2

Future Sounds Update, p.35

David Garibaldi

PERMUTATION STUDY #13.2 (CONT.)

2000 EE-LeVin V.2

2000 EE-Levin - Part 1: Odd Time in 4/4

This two-part study highlights two of the most effective concepts I use in beat-building (along with permutation): *odd time within 4/4 and tripletization*. In my DVD, *Breaking the Code* (Hudson Music), I demonstrate how I use the idea of odd time in 4/4. Included in the accompanying PDF are ideas in 5, 7, 9 and 11. I gave them names to make them personalized "rudiments": 5-a-Diddles, 9-a-Diddles, 7-a-Diddles, 11-a-Diddles, etc. I use these ideas/rudiments in different ways to create beats and over time have expanded this approach, which I'll explain here.

Years ago, I became fascinated with this idea of playing odd time over or within 4/4, and have used this concept to open up my ability to create unusual grooves. I've always loved the funky groove, and playing odd-time music in general never excited me that much. But one day as I was experimenting with a groove in 7, and as I was playing and listening, the thought floated into my head to play this 7 within 4/4.

So I learned a beat in 7/8 and at the next TOP rehearsal, I tried it over the intro to a song called "Knock Yourself Out." As the groove cycled through 7, it accented different parts of the horn line, but in a very random way. It was very apparent that this was a powerful way to build grooves and phrases that were different than the more traditional way I had been using up to that point. To my ears, it sounded like James Brown with some beats missing—super funk!

Also at that time, I was just starting to understand that there's groove beyond 2 & 4. I wanted to somehow make music out of the weird beats I was hearing and make it groove. Songs like "What Is Hip?," "Soul Vaccination," "Oakland Stroke," "On the Serious Side," and others showed me that it was absolutely possible. This rhythmic freedom changed me and also the face of TOP—it changed us from a garage soul band into something much more; something that is still growing and redefining itself.

Over time, I've assembled a toolbox that has allowed me to put my ideas into action. This toolbox makes it possible for me to take all the different types of music I like and to create a personalized approach to my drumming.

Measures A-K are the 11/16 phrase, played within 4/4. This creates a cycle of 11 measures before coming back to where it starts. In my practice, I repeat this cycle many times, and count my way through until it eventually feels as if I'm in 4/4. Counting is very powerful and after a while, the groove does feel like James Brown with some beats missing: a very syncopated 4/4 groove.

Each bar of 11/16 is marked with a dashed line, showing where each phrase starts within 4/4. Once the perception of 4/4 is there, I like to isolate or combine individual measures to create "loops."

For example, on page 2 are measures A-C from the 11-bar cycle as one-bar grooves with slight modifications, plus measures A-B combined to make a two-bar phrase that substitutes LF/HH for RF/BD at the end as the phrase repeats. Other measures can be combined as well.

I modify the patterns to help me with repeating and connecting the end to the beginning, so there are no more than two notes on any limb, which happens with some of the measures. Of course, these measures can be played as written and combined in many ways. Experiment!

Because of the odd number of notes, the phrases often land in unusual places when playing them in a musical context. Also, these loops can be permutated by quarter notes or 16th notes, which develops them even further.

As I've said before, **counting** been a huge part in opening my understanding of rhythm. This is a key concept, and ignoring its importance is severely limiting. Counting is our GPS! I learned about the power of permutation through counting. The same applies to odd time in 4/4 and, in Part 2, tripletization.

I know that this all sounds very intellectual and textbook, but my goal is always to be musical and to make these unusual beats groove. Think "Sideways James Brown."

Over time you will become less restricted by bar lines. Lots of repetition and counting will get you to this place. After building the counting habit, it will become less necessary to always count, as your inner clock becomes activated. ***COUNT!***

2000 EE-levin
Part 1

David Garibaldi

2000 EE-levin Part 1 (cont.)

2000 EE-levin - Part 2: Tripletization

This concept really was a pleasant surprise. I don't remember when I began exploring this, but I've found it to be the crazy cousin of odd time in 4/4 and permutation. These three methods will take your groove playing to a powerful and very different place.

Here's how it works: Have you ever played single paradiddles as eighth-note triplets in 4/4? This is the same idea. Take any 16th-note pattern, in any time signature, and convert each 16th note to an eighth-note triplet. One 16th = One Eighth; the 16th notes become eighth-note triplets. Same groove or idea, just in a triplet rate. In *Future Sounds*, on pages 12-13, is a study on single paradiddles as 16th notes and also as eighth-note triplets.

4/4 = 12/8 = 2 bars of 6/8: the quarter note becomes a dotted quarter note. The beat remains the same, but now it's a triplet rate instead of 16th notes.

All that being said, not all grooves will sound good to your ears—you decide. Apply the concept and see what happens. There's room in this for everyone.

Compare Ex. 1, Part 1 with Ex. 1 Part 2 for a visual on how it looks. Then begin putting it together a measure at a time until you can play the complete cycle. **Count.** Once you're comfortable and it feels like 4/4, start isolating and/or combining measures.

On page 2, I've isolated and measures A/B, C/D, G/H and I/J. The slight modifications in A/B and I/J make the turnarounds flow more easily. Combining measures creates a different flow amongst the limbs. Lots of repetitions will make these comfortable and build muscle memory.

As a member of Talking Drums I had the opportunity to learn about and play many of these rhythms. I looked at it just like I do with Tower of Power, and began creating beats with triplets. My mind was blown at how well these worked with clave and fit with all the traditional 6/8 rhythms we played. In this music, 4/4 and 6/8 go back and forth. The basic pulse remains the same; just the rates change. Compositionally, it's equally as powerful as creating with 16th notes.

Let me say this again: **Counting** been a huge part in opening my understanding of rhythm. This is a key concept, and ignoring its importance is severely limiting. Counting is our GPS, it unlocks the power of permutation, odd time in 4/4, and now tripletization. Turn on your clock and ***count!***

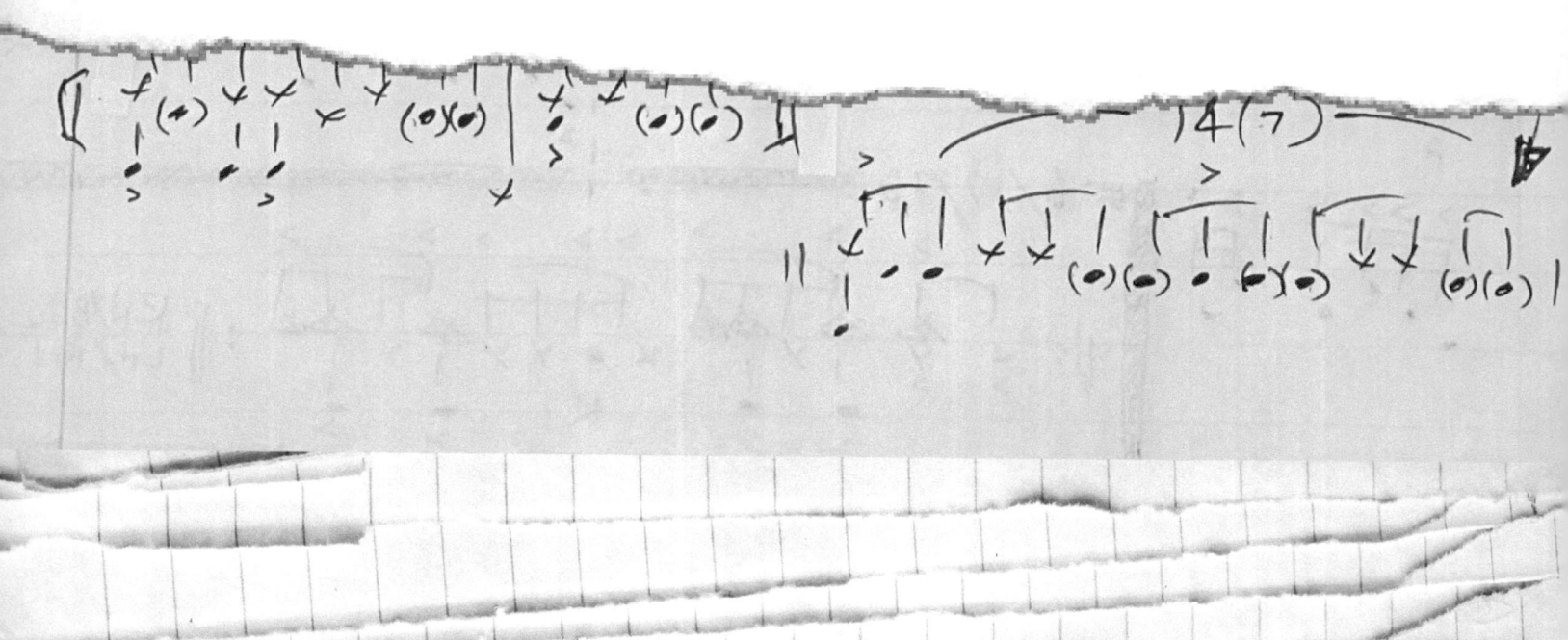

Drumz — David Garibaldi

2000 EE-levin
Part 2

♩ = ♩. = 100-110

2000 EE-levin Part 2 (cont.)

THE EAST BAY 13z

The East Bay 13'z

Continuing on with *odd time in 4/4 and tripletization*, here are my original notes from a practice session on January 5, 2018.

In this four-part study, let's look at 13/16. Although I've divided the study into four parts, there's so much to learn from this, it could be much more. Here are the basic ideas.

Part 1: The East Bay 13z in 4/4

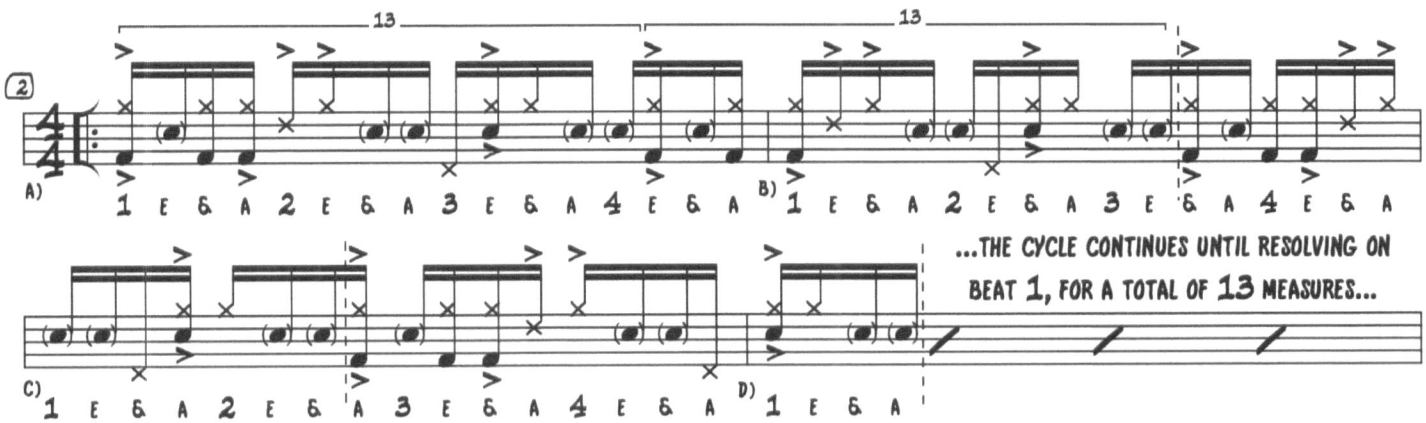

This is the 13/16 thirteen-measure cycle in 4/4. The following example illustrates the counting sequence 13/16 within 4/4: Each 13/16 phrase begins on a 16th note position in order, starting with the 1, then "e," then "&," then "a," eventually resolving to beat 1 after 13 total measures.

Part 2: Isolating and Combining Measures

These are the individual component measures in the cycle, played separately or combined to make longer phrases. Some of the stickings are modified slightly to enhance the flow of rights and lefts when repeating and connecting the measures.

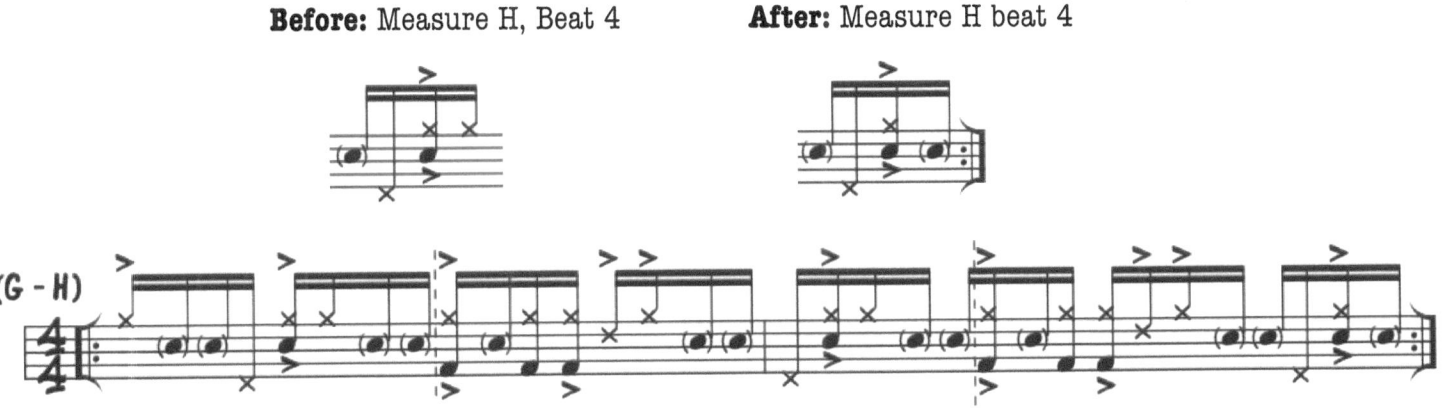

Part 3: The East Bay 13z in 4/4 as Triplets

Tripletizing the 13/16 sequence turns the phrase into 13/8: one 16th note = one eighth note. The same conversion process used with 11/16 is utilized here. Each 13/8 phrase begins on an eighth note position in the triplet order, starting with the 1, then "&," then "a," and eventually resolving to beat 1 after 13 total measures.

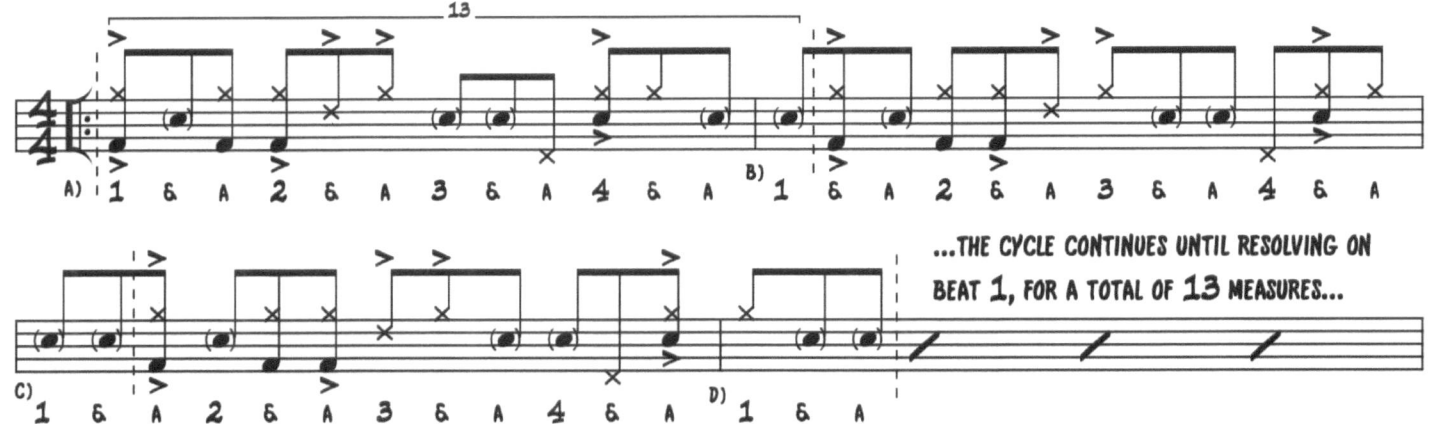

Part 4: Isolating and Combining Measures

The same idea as in Part 2: isolate and combine measures to create additional grooves. Watch for slight modifications in the stickings; sometimes when isolating measures, there could be three notes in a voice when repeating.

Wherever this happens, I substitute another voice so that there are no more than two notes with any limb. These following two examples can be played separately or connected as a two-bar phrase.

Here's an example of a two-bar combination. On the combined grooves page here in Part 4, you'll find several others. Make up your own, there are lots of possibilities available!

COUNT!

As I've said before, **counting** is a key concept and transformative. Counting is our GPS and allows us to experience the rhythmic power and flexibility of permutation, odd time in 4/4, and now tripletization. Repetition and patience brings it all together. Enjoy!

The East Bay 13'z
Part 1

David Garibaldi

THE EAST BAY 13'z
Part 2

David Garibaldi

THE EAST BAY 13'z - Part 2 (cont.)

The East Bay 13'z
Part 3

David Garibaldi

The East Bay 13'z
Part 4

David Garibaldi

♩ = ♩. = 90-110

BD can be substituted for LF/HH

The East Bay 13'z (cont.)

(K - L - H - A)

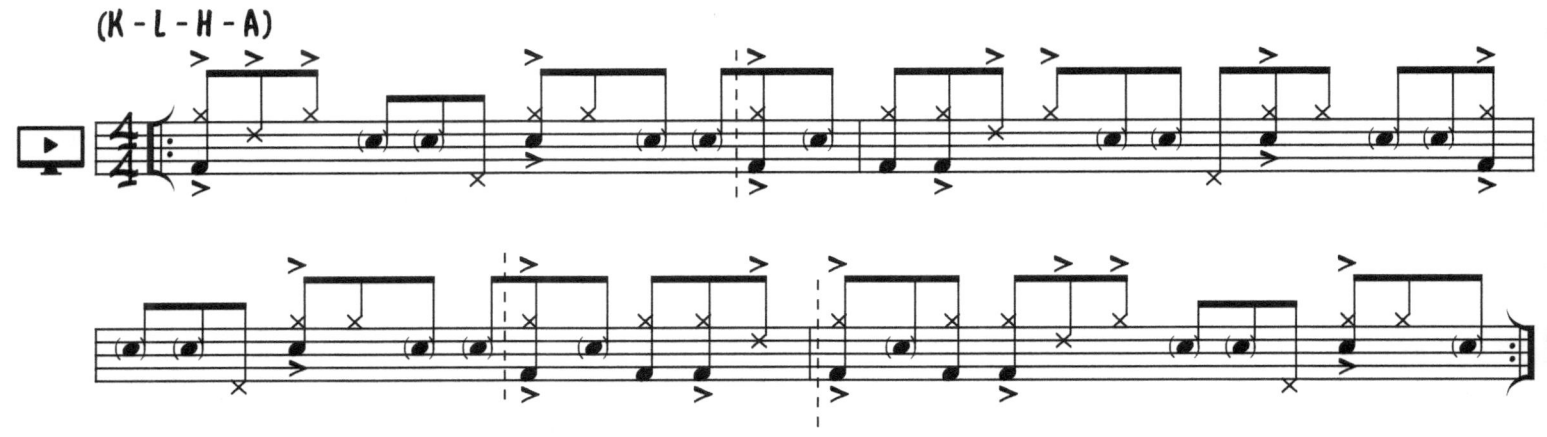

DG's Resource List

DG'z Resource List

In my previous books, I've always included a list of study materials that I've found to be very helpful. Some of the key books from previous suggestions remain, but along the way, new ones always appear. I suggest building a personalized study library that you can add or subtract from. As we get older, our study habits change and so do our resources. Here are a few; check out the Hudson website for many more: **HudsonMusic.com**

The Hands

- *Stick Control* - George Lawrence Stone
- *Master Studies* - Joe Morello
- *The All-American Drummer* - Charles Wilcoxon
- *Gaddiments* - Steve Gadd
- *Wrist Twisters* - Buster Bailey
- *Camp Duty Update* - Claus Hessler
- *The Rudimental Ritual* - Alan Dawson (Editor's note: the ritual is documented in John Ramsay's book *The Complete Drummer's Vocabulary as Taught by Alan Dawson*.)

The Feet

- *Secret Weapons for the Modern Drummer, Pt.2* - Jojo Mayer
- *Bass Drum Control* - Colin Bailey

The Head

- *Fearless* - Steve Chandler
- *Reinventing Yourself* - Steve Chandler
- *The Talent Code* - Daniel Coyle
- *Little Book of Talent* - Daniel Coyle
- *Talent is Overrated* - Geoff Colvin
- *Limitless* - Jim Kwik
- *The Practicing Mind* - Thomas M. Sterner
- *The Obstacle is the Way* - Ryan Holiday
- *The 5 Second Rule* - Mel Robbins

The Drums

- *The Brazilian Groove Book* - Kiko Freitas
- *Percussion Tutor* - Excellent loops to practice with, as well as a book.
- *Pathways of Motion* - Steve Smith
- *The Post-Bop Drum Book* - Mike Clark
- *Mastering the Tables of Time* - David Stanoch
- *West African Drumming, Books 1 & 2* - Mohktar Samba
- All of Gary Chaffee's books: Every time I pick one of these up, I learn something. (Editor's note: Gary's classic books are the *Patterns* series, consisting of 5 volumes, plus *Linear Time Playing*.)

About the Author

Born and raised in the San Francisco Bay Area, David began playing drums at the age of ten. At seventeen, he started his professional career, and in 1966 joined the United States Air Force where he became a member of the 724th USAF band stationed at McChord Air Force Base in Tacoma, Washington. Upon leaving the military in 1969, he returned to the Bay Area and on July 23, 1970, joined the legendary Tower of Power. It was in this setting that David became an innovator in funk drumming and one of the most influential drummers of his generation.

As a writer and performer, David has worked with Patti Austin, Natalie Cole, Mickey Hart's Planet Drum, Boz Scaggs, The BBC Orchestra, Gino Vannelli, Talking Drums, The Buddy Rich Orchestra, Ray Obiedo, Wishful Thinking, Poncho Sanchez, and many others. He is currently back recording and performing with Tower of Power after an eighteen-year hiatus.

David's awards and accolades include winning the *Modern Drummer* Readers Poll in the "Traditional R&B/Funk" category eight times, including five consecutive years from 1980-1985, then again in 2003, 2007, and 2009. His name now permanently resides in that poll's "honor roll" category for his lasting contributions to the percussive arts.

Considered a pioneering drum set educator, David's books and DVDs have won numerous awards, with *Future Sounds* being considered a classic standard of drum set pedagogy. David was on the percussion faculty at the Dick Grove School of Music in Los Angeles, California, from 1982-1989; has been an international clinician since 1980; was inducted into the Percussive Arts Society Hall of Fame 2012; has been Artist-in-Residence at the Drummers Collective in New York City and Accademia Musica Moderna in Milan Italy; and was presented with the Guitar Center Legends Award in 2008.

David proudly endorses Yamaha drums, Sabian cymbals, Vic Firth sticks, Latin Percussion, Remo drumheads, and Audix microphones.

Also By David Garibaldi

Educational DVDs:
- *David Garibaldi featuring Talking Drums*
- *David Garibaldi Tower of Groove: Complete*
- *Lessons: Breaking the Code*

Drum set instruction books:
- *Future Sounds*
- *The Funky Beat*
- *TimbaFunk* (Talking Drums, featuring Michael Spiro and Jesús Diaz)
- *Tiempo* (Talking Drums, featuring Michael Spiro and Jesús Diaz)
- *The Code of Funk*
- *Off the Record*

Drum Loop CD: *Tower of Funk Classic Funk and R&B Drum Loops*